Contents

Department of the Environment
The Welsh Office

'A Background
Water Reorga
'in England an

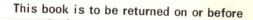
London: Her Majesty's Stationery Office 1973

© Crown copyright 1973

SBN 11 750570 6

Foreword

By the Secretaries of State for the Environment and for Wales

The Government are presenting to Parliament a Bill to reorganise water services in England and Wales. This reorganisation will bring together, under new multi-purpose authorities, responsibilities for water conservation and supply; sewerage and sewage disposal; the control of water pollution; land drainage and flood prevention; recreation, fisheries and in some cases inland navigation.

The Bill has been prepared following an exhaustive process of consultation. The Central Advisory Water Committee reported on "The Future Management of Water in England and Wales" early in 1971. The Government's conclusions on the Committee's recommendations were announced in December 1971. Since then, the Government Departments concerned have issued some seventeen consultation papers on the many aspects of the proposals. The comments on these papers have been very carefully considered and taken fully into account in the preparation of the Bill.

In addition, we thought there was a need for a document which brought together all the many aspects of water management, summarised the progress made so far in the development of the different functions of the new authorities and made clear the problems which remain to be resolved. To assist Parliament in considering the Bill, we therefore asked our Departments, in association with the Ministry of Agriculture, Fisheries and Food, to prepare this report. Little of its content is new, but the material is drawn together in a single place for the first time, and illustrates the inter-dependence of the many aspects of the "water cycle".

Apart from its value to Parliament as a background to reorganisation, we are confident that it will be of interest to a wider public — not only to the existing authorities and their successors, but also to the public at large. We hope it will help to illuminate this little known area of our economy, and to encourage public discussion on the many problems we face for the rest of the century and beyond.

GEOFFREY RIPPON
Secretary of State
for the
Environment

PETER THOMAS
Secretary of State
for
Wales

I Objectives

1 The Government have put forward proposals* for the reorganisation of water services in England and Wales. These envisage the formation of ten regional water authorities, to take over the existing functions of river authorities, water undertakers, sewerage and sewage disposal authorities. The Government have announced their intention to present the necessary legislation in the 1972/3 session of Parliament.

2 The new authorities will be responsible for meeting the various demands on river systems, and on water resources in the widest sense, and thus for adopting an integrated approach to river management, embracing the wide range of functions for which the present authorities are responsible. This report examines each of these functions; reports on the progress on them which the existing authorities have already made; and discusses the further measures which have already been proposed and the areas where important decisions remain to be taken. Before considering the individual functions, however, it is important to clarify the objectives they are designed to meet.

3 Policy for water services must be designed to meet the needs of the community. Broadly, these may be summarised as follows:—

a A sufficient quantity of water for the community's requirements. A certain minimum is essential to protect public health. A great deal more is needed to support the modern economy and, further, to promote personal comfort and convenience (eg for washing machines, car cleaning etc).

b The water must be of the appropriate quality for the purpose concerned. For public supply this normally means it must be wholesome. For industry or agriculture, the quality needed will depend upon the particular use involved. Frequently, water abstracted direct from a source is of sufficient quality for industrial cooling, irrigation etc. In other cases, eg where water is an important part of the industrial process, the maintenance of quality and the absence of particular elements, or the presence of others, may be essential to the quality of the product or to the effective working of the process.

c The resultant waste must be disposed of without damage to public health or the environment. This may mean discharge to the public sewer or to the nearest water course — and, in either event, ultimately via rivers and their estuaries to the sea.

d Adequate provision must be made for drainage of the land and for flood protection, including protection from estuary and sea flooding.

e The well-being and development of salmon and freshwater fisheries in our rivers and estuaries must be safeguarded.

f Where appropriate, the rivers and inland waterways must also meet the needs of navigation, including the carriage of freight.

g The consumer expects all these services to be reliable in both quality and quantity. The provision of his own "stand-by facilities" against the risk of unreliability would be expensive and in many cases impossible.

h Regard must also be had to the interests of the people and communities who may be affected by proposals for the development of water resources, such as reservoirs and other works.

i More generally, the amenity aspects are of growing importance. At worst, people expect rivers to pass through their area without causing a nuisance. At best they expect them to be a pleasant part of the local landscape which they may enjoy. In addition, there is a wide and growing range of recreational uses of rivers and other inland waters, which must be developed in a way that is compatible with other needs.

4 The broad objective is to meet these needs as far as practicable, with due regard to both cost and economy. In general, the cost of supplying water is comparatively low. For example the cost of supplying the water for a hot bath is only a fraction of the cost of heating it. The quantity of water available in the country is likely to be adequate to meet demands in the foreseeable future, but investment on a large scale will be needed to provide it in the right places and in the right quality. It is essential therefore that the costs of meeting the demand for water are fully taken into account by water users so that the best economic use of resources is made. Moreover, full account must be taken of local needs and circumstances — for example, of the extent to which water may be reused in a particular situation and to which the quality must be sustained for this purpose.

5 It must also be emphasised that these various uses of water are interdependent to varying degrees. The Government have therefore concluded that it is essential to adopt a multi-use approach, which is the basic reason for their proposals for the formation of Regional Water Authorities. There are also cases, however, where particular uses will conflict with each other, or where one use will limit — or at the extreme, may even preclude — another. For example, the use of a river as a source for public water supply might well limit the types of discharge that could be made to it upstream of the point of abstraction. Choices will have to be made. It is therefore an essential objective to ensure that, where this is the case, sufficient knowledge

* "Reorganisation of Water and Sewage Services: Government Proposals and Arrangements for Consultation" DOE Circular 92/71 HMSO 1971.

is available to the authorities to enable a rational choice to be made. Where research is necessary to achieve this, Government Departments and the new authorities will ensure that this is carried out. The proposed multi-purpose authorities should be able to take a broad view of all the functions involved and of the conflicting demands upon water resources and river management.

6 In the light of the needs discussed in the previous paragraphs, the Government's policy is designed to achieve the following major objectives:—

To secure an ample supply of water of appropriate quality to meet the growing demands of the people, industry and agriculture – while at the same time ensuring that it is not wasted.

To provide adequate sewerage and sewage disposal facilities to cope with the natural increase in water use and with new housing, industrial and agricultural developments.

To ensure that the vital contribution of land drainage and flood protection to both urban and agricultural areas alike is maintained and, where appropriate, expanded.

To achieve a massive clean up of the country's rivers and estuaries by the early 1980s.

To make the widest use of water space for other purposes, including recreation and amenity and, where appropriate, the protection and development of salmon and fresh-water fisheries and the provision of water needed for navigation.

To protect the interests of those who may be affected by proposals for the development of water resources in any of these respects.

II The Demand for Water

7 The Central Advisory Water Committee emphasised, in their report* "that the future development of water resources can best be planned over England and Wales as a whole"**. In order to achieve this, they recommended:

a The formulation of a *national plan* "to provide a strategy within which more detailed planning, and subsequently executive action, can proceed". They emphasised that this would need to cover the important questions of water quality, as well as quantity. The Committee considered that "there must be adequate opportunity for public debate about the issues involved. But once the strategy has been agreed, it must be regarded as a firm general commitment of Government policy, unless and until the periodic reviews show that changing circumstances have brought about the need for substantial modifications."

b *Regional plans* should be drawn up setting out what needed to be done in each region over a particular timescale.

c *Action programmes* would then be needed to ensure that the works required to implement the national and regional plan were constructed as and when they were needed. They would look to a shorter period than the national plan, and each programme would contain the works required in, say, the following five years, while indicating those expected to be needed in the five years after that, so that the necessary preparatory work could be done.

8 A good deal of work has already been done in this direction in relation to major conservation works. Section 14 of the Water Resources Act 1963 requires river authorities to survey the water resources in their areas. Substantial progress has been made in preparing and completing these surveys, though not all river authorities have yet finished the work. Meanwhile, the Water Resources Board, in close co-operation with the river authorities and the water supply industry, have reported on their three major studies of demands and resources in the South East, the North, and Wales and the Midlands respectively***. Each report examines a range of possible strategies for meeting the needs of the region concerned and concludes with recommendations on those schemes which might appropriately be followed up. Progress in following up these reports is summarised at the end of this chapter. Investigations have also been completed or are in hand on the possibility of storing water in a number of main estuaries or offshore sites: the Dee estuary, Morecambe Bay, the Solway Firth and the Wash*.

9 These various reports enable a view to be taken on a river basin or regional basis. For the reasons indicated above, it is essential to draw these together in a national strategy. The Water Resources Board are currently examining a range of possible strategies in a study of the water requirements of England and Wales as a whole. The results of the Board's study should be available early in 1973. Their work will have to be supplemented by further work on water quality, but it will provide an essential contribution to the process of forming a national water strategy.

10 It must be emphasised that this will be a strategy, not a fixed plan. It is essential to adopt a flexible basis for long term planning which can be reviewed and, if necessary, adapted in the light of developments and of new ideas, information and techniques. In the shorter term, "the principle must be to make firm recommendations for the near future which are at the same time logical steps in a wider long term strategy, itself susceptible to change"**. Moreover, it will be necessary to bring together planning work on water resources and water quality. On this basis, the proposals for reorganisation of water services, which are summarised in Chapter IX, should meet the recommendations of the Central Advisory Water Committee. It will be the job of the Department of the Environment and the Welsh Office, with the advice of the National Water Council, to develop the national strategy and to review it from time to time. Within that strategy, the Regional Water Authorities will be able to adopt regional plans and rolling capital investment programmes to ensure that the necessary developments are undertaken. Account will be taken during this process of the views of other interested parties, who will also have the same statutory rights to object to individual schemes when they are put forward as they have under the present law.

11 The basis of such planning, both nationally and regionally, must be an objective assessment of future demand and the examination and costing of both the economic and the social aspects of strategies for meeting it. The remainder of this chapter considers the growing demand for water and briefly describes the progress already made in implementing the recommendations in the three regional reports of the Water Resources Board. The following chapter examines the various methods which may be

---

* "The Future Management of Water in England and Wales", HMSO 1971.
** Chapter 4.
*** "Water Supplies in South East England" HMSO 1966.
  "Water Resources in the North" HMSO 1970.
  "Water Resources in Wales and the Midlands" HMSO 1971.

* "Dee Estuary Scheme" – Report by Binnie and Partners HMSO 1971.
  "Morecambe Bay: Estuary Storage" – Reports by the Board and by the Economic Study Group HMSO 1972.
  "Solway Barrage" – Report of Consultants and Report on Desk Study HMSO 1966.
  "The Wash: Estuary Storage" Report on Desk Study HSMO 1970.
** Fifth Annual Report of the Water Resources Board, paragraph 183. HMSO 1968.

available for meeting the demand in differing circumstances. Decisions on the development of a national strategy, however, cannot be taken until the Water Resources Board's national study is completed, and further studies are made on water quality, so that possible alternative strategies can be compared on a properly costed basis. The Government Departments will then begin the next stage in the task of drawing up an overall strategy, so that no time is lost when the new structure is introduced. Meanwhile, it will be necessary for detailed investigation, planning and implementation of particular projects to continue, to avoid any loss of momentum during the period of reorganisation.

The future demand for water

12 In their regional reports, the Water Resources Board examined future growth in demand, distinguishing between public supply and direct abstraction by industry and agriculture. The following paragraphs summarise the Board's most recent assessment of future growth in demand for England and Wales as a whole. This assessment will be discussed in more detail in the Board's forthcoming national study.

13 It must first be emphasised, however, that forecasts of future growth cannot be precise, since they are based on elements which cannot be forecast precisely: the growth of population; the growth in the use of water per head of the population; and the growth of *net* use of water by industry. While they are based on analysis of historical trends and on the official forecasts of population growth and distribution, these projections should be regarded as working assumptions for planning purposes, which will need to be regularly reviewed and revised in the light of developments. Even if growth proves somewhat less rapid, however, it seems probable that demand will reach the level projected between the turn of the century and 2010.

14 *Public water supply undertakers* in England and Wales supplied an average total of 13.9 million cubic metres per day (m³/d) (3058 million gallons per day (mgd)) in 1970. About two thirds of this was for domestic use. Demand is expected to rise to 28 million m³/d (6160 mgd) by about the end of the century, about double the present level of public supply. The total reliable yield of the resources currently available to water undertakers, or already authorised for development for this purpose, is estimated to be about 18 million m³/d (3960 mgd). These therefore need to be increased by a further 10 million m³/d (2200 mgd), or about 55%, to meet this demand.

15 The bulk of *direct abstraction* is undertaken by industry. Only a small fraction of the water used by industry represents an absolute call on resources and this mainly consists of loss by evaporation in cooling circuits or by incorporation in the product. The remainder of the water abstracted by industry is returned to the river nearby as effluent, where there is normally water to dilute it. It may then be used again further downstream, possibly several times. The net impact of these sequential uses can be assessed only by detailed analyses of individual rivers, which for the most part have yet to be undertaken. The

future growth of this type of demand depends on the rate of industrial growth, changes in technology, future patterns of industrial location, the elasticity of demand in relation to charges and the success of measures to maintain or improve river quality.

16 The total quantity of water taken by direct abstraction in 1970 was about 32 million m³/d (7040 mgd), of which only a small proportion was for agricultural purposes. In view of the absence of information about the extent to which water is used and not returned, and about the uncertainties discussed in the previous paragraph, it is difficult to make a firm projection about the net growth of direct abstraction. It seems unlikely, however, that this would be greatly in excess of the growth in sewage effluent generated by the increasing demand on the public water supply, which would then become available for direct abstraction. Apart from this, a broad analysis of the location of industrial demand suggests it would be prudent to allow for about a further 2 million m³/d (440 mgd) for net growth in direct abstraction.

17 Taking public water supply and direct abstraction together, this suggests a total need for new water resources of about 12 million m³/d (2640 mgd) by about the end of the century. It is expected that about 3 million m³/d (660 mgd) could be provided from local sources, which will be suitable to meet local needs but not for deployment over a wide area. This includes some yields which will accrue from the re-use of water discharged as effluent to rivers. The net deficiency for which plans must be developed on a wider scale is therefore about 9 million m³/d (about 2000 mgd) by the end of the century.

Meeting the demand

18 In assessing the net increase in demand and the possible alternative strategies for meeting it, the Water Resources Board have undertaken three main regional studies. They first tackled the problems of the *South East of England*, which clearly emerged as one of the main problem areas. The report on the Board's study was published in May 1966. It was expected that the parts of the area along the South and East coasts should be able to meet foreseen demands from their own resources, but deficiencies were expected to arise within the central area. Even here, however, the Board concluded that the area as a whole could go a long way to meeting its demands until near the end of the century.

19 In order to tackle the problems identified in their report, the Board put forward a two-part programme. First, they listed projects on which immediate action was needed to secure the position for the following decade. Of these major projects:—

a The necessary orders have been made authorising a new intake to provide an increased yield from Grafham Water.

b The construction of Datchet Reservoir has been started, and is due for completion in 1974.

c The first stage of the Ely Ouse – Essex scheme was opened by Her Majesty the Queen in May 1971.

d The Sunnymeads intake on the River Thames is under construction and is due to be completed in 1974.

e Two of the local schemes in Essex and East Suffolk (Ardleigh Reservoir and the Cattawade Barrage) have been completed and an order has been made authorising construction of the Alton Water Reservoir.

The Empingham Reservoir is now also under construction.

20 Secondly, the Board proposed a programme of reconnaissance in depth to enable the longer term strategy to be determined. Most of the investigations recommended by the Board, including the groundwater pilot schemes in the Thames Valley and the Great Ouse area and the investigation of possible reservoir sites, have been completed and the first stage of the Thames Valley scheme has been approved. Studies of Lincolnshire groundwater, of storage in the Wash and of artificial recharge in Sussex and the London basin are in hand. The necessary material on projects for the South East – with the exception of the results of the investigation of the Wash – should therefore be available in time to be taken into account in the completion of the Water Resources Board's national study and the subsequent development of a national water strategy.

21 The Board's second report, on "Water Resources in the North", was published in February 1970. This examined a number of possible strategies for the region, and concluded that the main choice lay between a programme involving seven large reservoirs and an alternative programme in which a substantial proportion of the storage would be in Morecambe Bay and/or the Dee Estuary.

22 Once again, the Board recommended a twofold programme. First, they concluded that, to meet needs to the early 1980's a number of projects should be completed as soon as possible, and that others, including three important possible reservoir sites, should be investigated immediately. These investigations have now been completed. The Brenig reservoir has been approved and an inquiry has been held into the proposal for a reservoir at Kielder. The proposal for Farndale Reservoir was rejected by Parliament in 1971 when powers were sought in the Private Bill of the Yorkshire River Authority.

23 Secondly, the Board urged investigation of four other reservoir sites so that the programme involving inland storage could be considered on a comparable basis with that involving estuary storage. Investigations of these sites have now been completed, so that the North can also be fitted into the Board's national study.

24 The report on the Board's third regional study, on "Water Resources in Wales and the Midlands", was published in October 1971. The Board concluded that two crucial issues needed to be resolved by 1972/3 if a shortage of water was to be avoided in the late 1970s and early 1980s: the selection of a major source for further regulation of the Severn and of a source in the north Midlands. Secondly, the Board listed a number of other projects to be investigated in detail by 1975, so that a fully informed choice could be made to meet longer term demand. A programme of investigations is in hand, but the Secretary of State for Wales has indicated, following an earlier public inquiry, that he is not prepared to authorise investigations in the Dulas valley.

25 The Board have not undertaken a comprehensive study of South West England. This area will be largely self-sufficient in future and it is unlikely that links will be needed with other parts of the country. Further storage capacity will be needed to meet the increasing demands of Devon and Cornwall. Following rejection by Parliament of the proposal to construct a reservoir at Swincombe these needs have been considered by the Cornwall and Devon River Authorities. The Devon River Authority have applied for powers to construct a reservoir at Wimbleball, to supply west Somerset, north and east Devon and possibly also south west Devon. The Cornwall River Authority are expected to put forward formal proposals for their area in 1973.

26 The picture which emerges from the previous paragraphs is summarised in map 1 annexed to this report. This shows the areas in England and Wales which have the heaviest rainfall; the demand areas used in the WRB studies where net deficiencies are expected to arise before the end of the century; and the main sites where major reservoirs are under construction, or are under consideration.

III Methods of Meeting Demand

27 Two important points emerge from the analysis in the previous chapter. First, there will be a continuing need to augment water resources on a substantial scale for a long time to come. Secondly, many of the main areas of growth are in those parts of England and Wales which either have a lower rainfall than elsewhere, or where in any case the main sources have already been, or are currently being, fully exploited. This means that it will be necessary to pursue schemes which, taken together, involve some transfers of major quantities of water from source to point of use. This does not mean that it will be necessary to construct a "national water grid". But there will be a general tendency to need to move water — whether by pipeline or regulated river — both eastwards and southwards from the areas of heavy rainfall to areas of lower rainfall and higher demand — just as Birmingham, for example, already draws supplies from Wales. While much of this movement will be within the boundaries of the new regional authorities, there may need to be a limited number of movements across their boundaries which could involve substantial quantities of water. These factors emphasise the need to plan on both a national and a regional basis.

28 The present chapter discusses the main methods being examined for meeting the demand. Each will need to be considered on its merits in relation to the local circumstances in the areas concerned. Situations may well arise where the demand can best be met by a combination of two or more of these various methods. Before considering them, however, two points need to be emphasised. First, we are dependent upon the natural resources which nature provides through the water cycle. Apart from desalination (which if economic might offer prospects of using water directly from the sea), we are dependent upon the run-off from natural rainfall which becomes available for use in rivers or underground aquifers. Secondly, there is no painless way of supplying greatly increased quantities of water without undertaking major works. With the possible exception of desalination, it will be necessary to store water, either on the surface or underground, until it is needed for use; and in any event we shall need ways of transferring it from the point of storage (or, in the case of desalination, the point of production) to the point of use, which may be a considerable distance.

Local sources

29 Comparatively small local sources remain to be exploited in many areas. They are taken into account in the regional studies of the Water Resources Board, and in the forecast of net deficiencies of future supply in Chapter II. Their use is being examined and, where appropriate, developed by the existing authorities, and this will be continued by the new Regional Water Authorities. There are limits to the extent to which they may be used, however, without risk of prejudicing the supplies of existing users or, in coastal areas, of saline intrusion into groundwater sources. Where such resources do not exist — or, at any rate, not in sufficient quantities — more ambitious schemes will be needed.

River regulation

30 River authorities are increasingly seeking to augment, or make better use of, resources by river regulation. This involves the use of major water storage which can be replenished when rainfall is plentiful and river flow is high, and from which water can be released at times of low flow in the river, for abstraction further downstream. The primary purpose of this technique is to increase the yield for water supply, but by increasing the minimum flows in regulated stretches fisheries and amenity can also be improved.

31 Various sources may be used for this purpose. The most obvious is a major reservoir, such as the Clywedog reservoir which was constructed to regulate the flow of the river Severn. Most of the reservoirs put forward for consideration in the Water Resources Board's reports would be operated on this basis. In some cases, reservoirs originally constructed for direct supply are now likely to be converted wholly or partly to river regulation. Powers are being sought, for example, to use the compensation water from the Ladybower reservoir on the river Derwent for this purpose. Similarly the Water Resources Board have proposed the enlargement of the Craig Goch reservoir (which stores water in the Elan Valley for supply to Birmingham), so that it could be used to regulate both the Severn and the Wye.

32 Rivers may also be regulated from other sources. In some areas, for example, there is considerable further scope for the development of *underground sources.* The Secretary of State has approved a scheme submitted by the Thames Conservancy for the first stage of a development of this kind in the Thames Valley and the Great Ouse River Authority are considering the scope for it in the Great Ouse basin. Periodic low river flows would be augmented by pumping from the aquifer, which would be replenished by rainfall when river flow was naturally high and could sustain the yield. While this may involve discharging comparatively clean water into the river which would then subsequently require treatment when abstracted downstream, this approach may in some circumstances represent the most economic use of resources. The use of underground storage — whether of water naturally percolating to an aquifer or water reaching it by artificial recharge (which

is discussed in paragraph 35 below) — is more fully examined in the Water Resources Board's annual report for 1968/9*.

33 River regulation may also facilitate the *re-use of water*. Water is in practice already used several times during its passage from the headwaters to the sea. For example, sewage effluent may be discharged into a river where it is diluted by the natural river flow; and water, which contains a proportion of such effluent, is then abstracted from the river at a point downstream and either used directly by the abstractor or treated for public supply. There is scope for considerable increase in this, but this will depend to some extent upon progress in dealing with the problems discussed in Chapter IV. By evening out river flows, and in particular increasing them at times when they would normally be low, river regulation will be of great importance in the dilution process, on which such re-use depends.

Conjunctive use

34 The term "conjunctive use" is used to describe schemes which involve the use of two or more sources of supply — usually one in normal circumstances and the other at time either of peak demand or of a shortage of water from the normal source. A major example is the Lancashire conjunctive use scheme, which is being planned on a co-operative basis by the Lancashire River Authority and the Fylde Water Board. In this scheme abstractions from the River Lune would be balanced at times of low river flow by abstractions from the Bunter aquifer and supplies drawn from Stocks reservoir. Similarly, it is sometimes suggested that desalination plant (which is discussed in paragraphs 37-41 below) might be used on a conjunctive basis. Such schemes enable advantage to be taken of seasonal characteristics or other differences in the yield of different sources. It may well be practicable to apply the principle by associating different areas where such characteristics can be suitably matched.

Artificial recharge

35 The possibility of artificial recharge of aquifers is also under investigation. This involves feeding water into the aquifer at a time when it is plentiful, to make more use of its storage capacity than would be possible by natural recharge alone. Recharge may take place by water percolating through the bottom of a basin into the aquifer or through recharge boreholes assisted by pumping. Artificial recharge increases the amount of water available to be drawn off in times of shortage without requiring surface storage. It is used extensively in Holland, where circumstances are favourable, but its use in England and Wales may be limited by geological conditions in the areas concerned. Considerable research is needed both into the practicability of artificial recharge in particular localities and into the water quality aspects — there are risks, for example, of polluting the water in the natural aquifer by impurities in the recharge water or of elements in the aquifer affecting the water used for recharge. The Water Resources Board are investigating the feasibility and scope for artificial recharge by various means and have a number of pilot schemes. The Water Research Associa-

tion has a 5 year programme on aspects such as the effects of recharge rate on water quality and clogging during recharge. Further progress in the use of this technique depends upon the results of this work.

Estuary storage

36 Estuary storage schemes would enable water to be stored in large quantities in estuaries without using any significant amount of good agricultural land. For example, the Water Resources Board's report on "Water Resources in the North" suggested that estuary storage in Morecambe Bay might yield over 2 million m^3/d (440 mgd), which is more than twice the yield of the largest inland reservoir considered in the report. The scope for such developments will be fully explored in the Water Resources Board's national study. In addition to the practicability and cost of such schemes, the amenity, ecological and other aspects must be taken fully into account. Indeed, estuary storage is often conceived as one aspect of proposals for major estuarial developments. For example, in the work on the Dee and Morecambe Bay the scope for road crossings was examined, as well as water storage. Decisions on estuary storage must also take account of the quality of water reaching the lower stretches of rivers and the consequent treatment problems. If estuary schemes are incorporated in a national strategy, it is already clear that it will be desirable to keep the storage area separate from the normal river flow, so that the quality of water pumped to storage can be controlled.

Desalination

37 *Desalination* is often suggested as a way of supplying water without involving the construction of reservoirs. Again, the potential is being fully explored. Unfortunately, no desalination system is yet anywhere near competitive for UK conditions. In their report in 1969*, the Water Resources Board examined the known technology, taking into account the feasibility and economic studies of the Water Research Association, and came to the conclusion that, in general, the cost of producing fresh water by desalination processes was between two and three times that of normal water supply.

38 Following that report, the Board were advised by the United Kingdom Atomic Energy Authority** that the development of the secondary refrigerant process had reached a stage which would justify building a pilot plant, and that the cost of water produced by the process might be competitive in some situations with that of water from conventional sources. In order to test this possibility, the Board proposed, jointly with the AEA, to construct a pilot plant at Ipswich. This was approved by Ministers in March 1972, at an estimated cost to the Exchequer of £2 million. A contribution was also to be made by the industrial firm developing the process. In late 1971, however, the firm concerned decided they could not continue to contribute towards the project as they no longer foresaw any reasonably early return on their investment. It also became apparent that, since March 1971, there had been increases in the estimated costs of the project. In January 1972, on

---

* Sixth Annual report of the Water Resources Board HMSO 1970 Chapter 4.

* Report on Desalination for England and Wales HMSO 1969.
** See Appendix, paragraph 15.

the advice of the Water Resources Board, the Government decided not to proceed with the project.

39 Following this decision, the Secretary of State for the Environment asked the Water Resources Board to advise on further prospects for the secondary refrigerant process, and on the prospects for desalination generally, for water supply in England and Wales. The Board's report was presented to Ministers in October 1972*. It concluded that the research and development work undertaken for the Ipswich project had confirmed the technical potential of the secondary refrigerant process, but that the substantial cost advantage over other processes forecast in 1969 had not been realised. On the wider question, the report concluded that since 1969 the estimated cost of water from desalination had increased considerably more than that of water from conventional sources. In these circumstances, the Board are unable to forsee any substantial contribution being made by desalination to water resources in England and Wales before the end of the century, apart possibly from small local applications where the additional cost might be judged worthwhile.

40 The Board's report also emphasised that desalination plant is, no less than conventional sources, open to objection on environmental grounds. A plant big enough to supply water in any substantial quantity would resemble a petro-chemical installation, though on a smaller scale, and its visual impact would be severe. Some processes are noisy, particularly those using large compressors. Distillation or secondary refrigerant plant producing fresh water from sea water would need to be sited on parts of the coast which are relatively free from industrial development, to avoid excessive pollution of the feedwater. There could also be problems in disposing of the reject brine, which usually has at least twice the salinity of the feed stream. Moreover, the adoption of desalination would involve a major change from taking full advantage of natural resources and natural forces – solar distillation, rainfall and gravity – with comparatively marginal human interference to a method which relies heavily on the consumption of power, one of our scarcest resources.

41. So far, there has therefore been no change in the position that desalination plant could only be introduced in the UK at a considerable increase in cost of water supplies. Indeed, it now seems less likely than it did in 1969. The Government has encouraged research projects which offer any hope of changing this situation. The Water Resources Board have concluded, in their recent report, that a major research and development programme on desalination processes for water supply purposes in England and Wales cannot at present be justified ; but that experimental work on new processes should continue and a small research and development capability should be retained. This capability is already provided by the UKAEA**. Meanwhile, contacts are being pursued with those countries in Western Europe with similar problems, to explore the practicability and potential benefit of collaborative research in this field. Research is also continuing into the use of some desalination processes on other aspects of the water cycle, eg in water treatment and sewage treatment.

Regional and inter-regional schemes

42 As Chapter II made clear, schemes will need to be considered in relation to a wide area. There is nothing new in this. Birmingham has drawn supplies from the Elan Valley in Wales, Liverpool from North Wales and Manchester from the Lake District for generations. In these older schemes, the water is carried by aqueduct for direct supply to the area of demand. With river regulation, however, the river itself is used as a water carrier, the water being abstracted for treatment and supply downstream. Alternatively, another convenient watercourse may be suitable. For example, the Fossdyke Canal is being used in the Trent-Witham-Ancholme scheme, which will supply non-potable water from the Trent to industry in north Lincolnshire. Similarly, a system now links the Ely Ouse with the Essex rivers, Stour and Blackwater, enabling water to be transferred from the Ouse at Denver via existing rivers and watercourses, plus 12 miles of tunnel and 15 miles of pipeline, to reservoirs in Essex.

Influences on demand

43 The range of methods surveyed in the previous paragraphs relates to a situation where a demand exists, or may be anticipated, and needs to be met. As suggested earlier in this report, however, it may also be practicable in some cases to attempt to influence the demand itself.

44 Supply costs are comparatively low and water often appears to be used as if it were free. Apart from the re-use of water*, it may be practicable to discourage waste. To some extent, this might be achieved if charges reflected costs more closely, particularly for industrial users who are already charged according to quantity consumed, whether from public supply or by direct abstraction. Too little is known yet about the most economic way to use water, for example by recycling, but there are many successful examples where demand has been reduced in industrial processes or power stations. This may reduce the net demand, and/or reduce the quantity of water which is ultimately returned either to the public sewers, or alternatively to a watercourse but at a poorer quality and/or a higher temperature than it was taken out. For example, the report of the unofficial working party on the management of natural resources (which was set up to collect public opinion in preparation for the United Nations Conference on the Human Environment in Stockholm)**, pointed out that average consumption in steel manufacture is 37 tons of water for every ton of finished steel. Recycling can bring this to as low as 4 tons. The scope for this trend may be limited, however, to the extent that re-use of water in particular circumstances may result in the production of effluents or sludges which are more difficult to treat.

45 It may also be possible to vary the quality of water supplied. For example, there are some 30 water undertakings in England and Wales offering a dual supply to

* "Desalination 1972" HMSO 1972.
** See Appendix, paragraph 15.

* See paragraph 33.
** "Sinews for Survival", paragraph 122, HMSO 1972.

industry, one of potable and one of lower quality. Where it is economic to do so, this practice may develop further – though the cost of duplicating pipework will limit the scope for it. Even where it is economic, problems of water quality must be borne in mind. For example, adequate safeguards must be built in to a dual supply system to avoid the two supplies becoming interconnected, so that the potable water cannot be contaminated by that of lower quality; and to avoid the non-potable supply being used for an unsuitable purpose.

Reservoirs

46 The various studies completed or in hand which form essential steps in the development of a national strategy will take account of the possibilities reviewed in the previous paragraphs. It may be possible to avoid the construction of some further reservoirs by the enlargement of existing reservoirs or their transfer from direct supply to river regulation; or by other methods discussed in this Chapter. But a limited number of new reservoirs is still likely to be needed.

47 The acquisition of land for water resources developments, and particularly for major reservoirs, is often controversial, especially because of the effect it can have on local communities – often small communities in rural areas. Due regard must therefore be given to the interests of those likely to be affected, compared with such factors as the need for the reservoir to meet the demand for water over a wider area, the availability of other ways of meeting this and the relative economic and social costs. In some cases, reservoirs may be proposed on farming land. An important objective is to avoid or minimise the use of good agricultural land and the breaking up of farms. As has been pointed out, however, some of the alternative means will themselves be open to objection from landowners, amenity interests, those concerned with the ecology of the area, and so on. Within the national strategy, it will therefore be necessary to pursue some proposals which are shown to be practicable and economic and which avoid, or at least minimise, any hardship which may arise from reservoir construction. In some cases, a reservoir may provide an attractive feature of the countryside. The unofficial working party on the management of natural resources concluded that "there is nothing inherently wrong with reservoirs if sufficient care is taken over the selection of sites and their landscaping".* It is intended to ensure that the necessary steps are taken to achieve this. Reservoirs are often a source of enjoyment and relaxation to many people. The Derwent reservoir in Northumbria and the Chew reservoir in Somerset show what can be achieved. The extent to which the recreational potential of a reservoir can be developed, for example for fishing, sailing, boating etc depends among other things on the nature of the area. Chapter VII describes the Government's proposals to make the best use of water space for recreation and amenity.

48 Apart from these general issues, however, three particular areas of difficulty arise. The first is to secure

---

* "Sinews for Survival", paragraph 127.

satisfactory *compensation* for the owners and tenants of land which needs to be acquired for development. The Secretaries of State for the Environment, Scotland and Wales published a White Paper "Development and Compensation – Putting People First" (Cmnd 5124) in October 1972 setting out their proposals for amending the law of land compensation. The general improvements proposed include the right to an advance payment of 90% of the agreed or estimated compensation on or after entry; special home loss payment for householders who have lived in their homes for 7 years or more; improvements in the blight provisions; and new provisions for rehousing of residential occupiers. As indicated in paragraph 47, particular problems arise where agricultural land is involved. In addition to the general provisions, the White Paper makes specific proposals in this respect. These include a proposal that dispossessed owner-occupiers of agricultural units who move to a new farm should be entitled to a special payment in respect of the initial loss of profits incurred in farming unfamiliar land; owner-occupiers who lose part of their farms will be entitled to require enlargement of notice to treat in certain circumstances and a similar right will apply in respect of blight notices served by owner-occupiers. Tenants will be given a parallel right to require enlargement of notices of entry. These provisions should help to relieve a number of the problems which may be involved in promoting future reservoir schemes. The Land Compensation Bill embodying these proposals is now before Parliament.

49 Secondly, particular difficulties arise if reservoirs are proposed in *national parks.* Being mainly in wet, upland areas and usually with clean rivers, the parks provide, from the water point of view, good sites for reservoirs and there is normally little risk of pollution. The national parks comprise about 9% of the total land area of England and Wales and the provision of new reservoirs or the enlargement of existing ones in them cannot be totally ruled out. Among the factors to be taken into account here, as elsewhere, are the effect on communities, the environmental location, the agricultural value of the land, the recreational potential and the cost. But in addition any such developments must be compatible with the general aims and objectives of designating a particular area as a national park, and before approving the siting of any reservoir in a national park the Secretary of State, who will take into account the views of the Countryside Commission, will need to be convinced that all reasonable alternatives have been explored and that there are the strongest arguments for the proposal. Moreover, any such proposal requiring an order under the Water Resources Acts 1963–71 is subject to negative resolution procedure in either House of Parliament.

50 Thirdly, controversy often arises when river authorities wish to investigate sites which may be suitable for reservoirs. As Chapter II illustrates, authorities often wish to investigate a number of possible sites before deciding which appears most suitable for development. Indeed, in the past, river authorities have been criticised for failing to do this. It is understandable that those living in, or interested in, the areas concerned may wish to resist such proposals, and that they may object to the effects

which may arise from the investigation of a site which is subsequently not selected for development. On the other hand, it is important to distinguish between the *investigation* of the suitability of a site, and proposals for the *construction* of a reservoir. If a rational choice is to be made, as proposed elsewhere in this report, investigations will be needed of more sites than will need to be developed, but full information is needed if a proper and fair judgment is to be possible.

51 It is arguable that objection at the investigation stage may not help those who might be affected by eventual development. If compulsory powers of investigation are nevertheless granted, this will only be after the elapse of time involved in a public inquiry and the consideration of an inspector's report by Ministers – this will normally take longer than the investigations themselves. Secondly, if after investigation a site is proposed for development, the case for or against the reservoir will have been considered at length at two public inquiries. Thus the period during which a site is blighted may be increased and, if the site is proposed for development, this may involve objectors in the expense of preparing evidence twice on the same issue. In some cases, these difficulties have been reduced when objectors have been prepared to agree to the investigation of sites without prejudice to their right to object to subsequent development.

52 Last, it is essential to ensure that reservoirs do not endanger public safety. Their construction and maintenance is at present governed by the *Reservoirs (Safety Provisions) Act 1930.* Its operation has been reviewed by the Institution of Civil Engineers, who have put forward proposals for strengthening it. The Government have agreed that changes are needed to strengthen the operation of the Act, and propose to introduce the necessary legislation as soon as possible.

IV Water Quality

53 Chapter I indicated that one of the objectives of water policy is to ensure that the water user is able to obtain water of the quality he needs for the purpose for which he wishes to use it. Quality can only be assessed in relation to use. For example, water which is quite suitable for industry might well be quite unsuitable for domestic purposes. It is also important to differentiate between the use of water as it occurs naturally, eg for the maintenance of fish and wildlife or for recreation and amenity in lakes and rivers, and the use of water after processing. An industry or a water undertaking can usually compensate for a poorer quality source of water by more extensive treatment, although this entails higher costs. Conversely, it is an uneconomic use of resources to use water of a much higher quality than the minimum needed for the purpose. There are many instances in which this occurs.

54 Considerably more effort needs to be devoted in future to problems relating to water quality. In the past, water supplies have been abundant and until recently there have been no great difficulties in meeting demand, except in a few localities. It has therefore been possible for water supply undertakings to seek the purest supplies of water for their consumers. As demand grows, this is becoming increasingly difficult. As was made clear in Chapter III, the national strategy must deal with a situation where much of the rain falls some distance away from the main centres of demand, and large quantities of water will need to be moved for considerable distances. If rivers used as carriers also receive effluent, this could impair the water quality. Similarly, quality problems may arise from increasing use of river regulation. But the growing demand also means that there has been — and will continue to be — a trend towards the use for supply of lower quality sources than in the past. All this has two main implications. First, we need to be sure that the water when supplied is wholesome, to avoid risk of causing harm, particularly to public health. Secondly, where it is economic to do so, it may be desirable to avoid supplying water of a higher quality than is strictly needed. For these reasons, the water quality aspects must be taken fully into account in water resources planning.

Gaps in knowledge

55 First, however, considerably more needs to be known about problems related to water quality. In the present state of knowledge, because of the multiplicity of factors involved, no-one can define with any precision all the elements of an appropriate standard of water quality for a particular purpose. This is not simply a question of setting the highest standards for the supply of water. As was pointed out by the working party on the control of pollution (another of the unofficial working parties set up to report on public opinion in preparation for the United Nations Conference on the Human Environment) "extremely pure water is hardly able to support any aquatic life at all. This is because it lacks phosphates, nitrates and assimilable carbon, which are essential to plants and animal growth"*. Not merely does extremely pure water lack such nutrients, many people would find it unpalatable. It is possible, for example, to produce water which is so pure that it needs to be mixed with less pure water to provide a palatable taste. For these reasons, it is important to find out more than we know at present about the desirable composition of water for particular uses.

56 At the other extreme, there are elements which may be harmful, either when present in the river itself, or if contained in water which is abstracted for use. Until recently, treatment processes have been designed to deal with domestic sewage and the effluents from relatively simple industrial processes with the object of preventing the spread of water-borne disease and preventing rivers from becoming foul. These processes reduce oxidisable and suspended matter but some bacteria and viruses remain and, if water is to be re-used for potable supply, these must be inactivated or removed by water treatment. More recent years have seen an increase in the scale of industry and, perhaps more important, in the variety and complexity of the substances manufactured. Even after treatment the effluents from such processes may contain very small amounts of unknown, and therefore possibly hazardous, substances. The problems of identifying such substances and assessing their effects are numerous and complex. It is necessary to consider indirect effects via the food chains of plants and animals as well as any direct effects on human health. There are also difficulties of chemical analysis, for while with modern equipment small traces of most elements can readily be measured, there are intractable problems in dealing with traces of organic compounds whose composition is unknown.

57 There are other examples of problems which may arise from composition of the water. There is a statistical association between the consumption of soft water and the incidence of cardiovascular disease. Excessive concentrations of nitrate in water can be particularly harmful to children in their first year of life. High concentrations of ammonia in river water interfere with disinfection by chlorine of water abstracted for public supply. Much has still to be learned about the importance and, in some cases, possible harmful effects of trace elements and

---

* "Pollution: Nuisance or Nemesis?", paragraph 88 HMSO 1972.

other trace substances in water supplies.

58 Lastly, there are risks of contamination of water after it has been taken into supply, or even after it has been treated. For example, reservoirs close to a road may be affected by spillages from vehicles on the road; or treated water may be affected by action within the supply system, eg from passing through lead pipes.

Water quality standards

59 In this country the responsibility for providing a wholesome supply of water is placed by law directly and in general terms on the statutory water undertakers, the word "wholesome" implying inter alia that the supply must be safe. The decision whether or not the water is wholesome would, in the final resort, be determined by the courts, but in practice water undertakers rely on the advice of their professional staffs and consultants and on that of the Medical Officer of Health who has a responsibility for ensuring that all measures are taken to protect the health of the population in his area. In determining the wholesomeness of a water, a statutory undertaking will have regard to published works of authority including, in particular, the World Health Organisation's International Water Standards and their European Water Standards, together with the "Bacteriological Examination of Water Supplies" published jointly by the Department of Health and Social Security, the Welsh Office and the then Ministry of Housing and Local Government in 1969 (3rd Edition). The absence of any formal standards laid down by Regulation has been regarded as advantageous since the figure for any particular constituent of a water may be raised or lowered in accordance with the results of new research without having to wait for the revision of a statutory instrument. Moreover, the circumstances of individual supplies may sometimes have to be taken into account in determining a practicable solution, as in the case of nitrate concentrations mentioned in paragraph 64. Nevertheless, except in special cases where the individual medical and other circumstances have been carefully assessed, the maximum allowable concentrations laid down in the WHO Standards should not be exceeded and in the case of toxic substances, such as many of the heavy metals, the actual concentrations should be kept as low as practicable.

60 Paragraphs 55-58 illustrate some of the more recent problems of water quality which are likely to become of greater importance in the future. They are not intended to cast any doubt upon the wholesomeness of present public water supplies or the success with which the public health and water supply authorities have carried out their responsibilities. It is, however, important to realise that the hazards are constantly changing and the safeguards must be continuously adapted to new situations.

61 As a step in seeking to do this, the Government established a Steering Committee on Water Quality, which produced its first report last year*. The Department of Health and Social Security has also established a new committee whose responsibilities go wider than matters affecting water, but which will be responsible for considering problems relating to possible effects of water quality on public health.

62 In the light of the work of the Steering Committee, three main steps need to be taken. First, in order to fill more of the existing gaps in knowledge, and to anticipate problems before they become serious, there is a need for more research on many aspects of water supply and pollution. Much of this is being undertaken at the Department's Water Pollution Research Laboratory and, with Government financial support, by the Water Research Association. The field of research may be extended as a result of the work of the Department of Health and Social Security's new committee dealing with the medical aspects of environmental contamination.

63 Secondly, the Steering Committee's technical panel is drawing up guidelines for water quality for public supply, industry, agriculture, fish and wildlife, and recreation and amenity respectively. These will not be in the form of recommended standard limits, but will indicate the various considerations to be taken into account in deciding what is appropriate in given local circumstances. They will then need to be developed in the light of further discussion and of knowledge arising from research. They should however provide a step towards firmer criteria than we have at present for the quality standards needed for the different uses under consideration.

64 Thirdly, it is essential to maintain a substantial safety margin, which should only be reduced where it is absolutely clear that it is safe to do so. The Steering Committee has itself recommended that "all new schemes for the abstraction of water from rivers should incorporate provision for the storage of raw water for at least seven days before treatment"*. This is intended to avoid the risk of accidental pollution, for example from transport, agricultural, mineral and land use activities. Another example relates to those limited areas where there is a higher nitrate concentration in the local water supply than may be desirable, even though below known danger levels. Where possible this problem is solved by mixing the high nitrate supply with one from a nearby source with a lower nitrate content; but it has been necessary in a few cases to make a supply of purer water available for infants and very small children.

65 As pointed out earlier, in some cases water is supplied at higher quality than is strictly necessary. For example, potable water is used in some cases in trade, industry or agriculture where water of this quality is not strictly necessary. For certain purposes, water of inferior quality is adequate and a dual supply system may sometimes be adopted at acceptable cost to conserve water of potable quality. In other cases existence of a cheap and plentiful source of water of potable quality may make this solution unnecessary or the cost of duplication of distribution mains may make its adoption expensive. Chapter III indicated some examples of measures to reduce either the overall demand for water or the demand for high quality water; the financial and economic problems are discussed further in Chapter IX.

---

* First Annual Report of the Steering Committee on Water Quality HMSO 1971.

* First Annual Report, paragraph 25.

V Water Pollution

66 The previous chapters have dealt with the use of rivers primarily for water supply. Their second main use is to carry away the liquid waste arising from domestic properties and from trade and industry. Volume 2 of the River Pollution Survey 1970* shows that the total daily flow of industrial effluent and domestic sewage to rivers and canals exceeds 21 million m³ (4500 mg), excluding cooling waters and discharges from mines. While rivers have a natural capacity for self-purification, they would be unable to absorb this quantity of sewage and other effluent without adverse effect if it were not treated before discharge. Moreover, rivers also have to cope with other polluting materials which may drain into them naturally, or which are deposited in them whether legally or illegally.

67 There are a number of reasons why it is essential to reduce pollution in our rivers. First, the water in many rivers is an essential part of the water supply. At the very least, pollution increases the cost of treating the water before it can be used. Much worse, it may make water resources unusable. Secondly, for the reasons outlined in Chapter IV, pollution may affect public health or safety in other ways. It can affect both plant and animal life in rivers, estuaries and the sea. This may directly reduce the food supply or the safety of foods for human consumption may be affected by the passing of harmful substances into water supplies or through food chains. The accumulation of sub-lethal amounts of certain persistent substances such as DDT and mercury can result in fish and other organisms being classified unfit for human consumption, without killing the organisms themselves. Thirdly, a seriously polluted river or estuary may be a public nuisance. For example, shorelines may become fouled by crude or partially treated sewage or fatty solids, or the river may smell. Fourthly, rivers and estuaries are a major source of marine pollution and it is becoming increasingly necessary to reduce all forms of pollution entering the sea. The UK has played a leading part in international work in this respect (described more fully in paragraph 82 below) and it is already clear that action will have to be taken to reduce river pollution in order to meet international obligations.

68 There are thus a number of risks which need to be avoided or minimised. But the public demand for rising standards in the environment calls for more than this. A properly managed river can provide a pleasant amenity with facilities for recreation.

69 This calls for a programme with three aims:
 To avoid any further deterioration of the quality of water in rivers.

 To remove the objectionable features arising from existing pollution, and to reduce that pollution.
 To enable the natural beauty of rivers to be properly appreciated and their recreational potential fully realised.

70 Legislation controlling river pollution dates back primarily to the 19th century (though some is much earlier). The present system of control has been developed in recent years. Discharges to the rivers are controlled by river authorities under the Rivers (Prevention of Pollution) Acts 1951-1961. Under this legislation, the authority's consent is required for discharges to non-tidal rivers*.

71 Volume 2 of the Report of the River Pollution Survey 1970 shows that over 10 million m³/d of effluent from sewage treatment works (about 18% of which is industrial effluent), 1.2 million m³/d of crude sewage, nearly 11 million m³/d of industrial effluent, 63 million m³/d of cooling water and 1 million m³/d of water from mines, are discharged into the rivers and canals of England and Wales. About 82% of domestic sewage is treated in disposal works, 12% is discharged direct to the sea and 6% disposed of by other means. About 16% of industrial effluents are discharged to the sea, 81% to rivers and 3% to sewage treatment works.

72 The 1970 River Pollution Survey**, and the further up-dating published more recently***, show the progress which has been made in improving river quality. An earlier survey — which was undertaken on a more limited basis — had shown that in 1958, while 14,000 miles of non-tidal river were unpolluted, over 2,500 miles were either in poor condition or grossly polluted. By 1970, over 17,000 miles were unpolluted and only 2,000 miles were in poor condition or grossly polluted. While it is not possible to make precise comparisons between the two surveys, there has clearly been some overall improvement. The report on the first up-dating of the 1970 survey shows a small but significant further improvement in the standards of the country's rivers as a whole, though some stretches of river have deteriorated. More than one mile in every ten classed as heavily polluted in 1970 by 1972 had been improved, with the result that there are 240 miles less of heavily polluted non-tidal stretches of river. The improvements shown by these three surveys are illustrated in the chart on page 20. But there is no room for complacency. There is considerable scope for further improvement. Monitoring should be on a more comprehensive basis. Arrangements have now been made for a regular up-dating of the main information in the survey, of which the

---

* HMSO 1972. Results were summarised in DOE Circular 64/72 (Welsh Office 127/72) HMSO.

 * For tidal rivers see paragraph 77 below.
 ** Report of a River Pollution Survey of England and Wales 1970 HMSO 1971.
 *** "River Pollution Survey of England and Wales Updated 1972 — River Quality" HMSO 1972.

RIVER QUALITY

Non – tidal Rivers

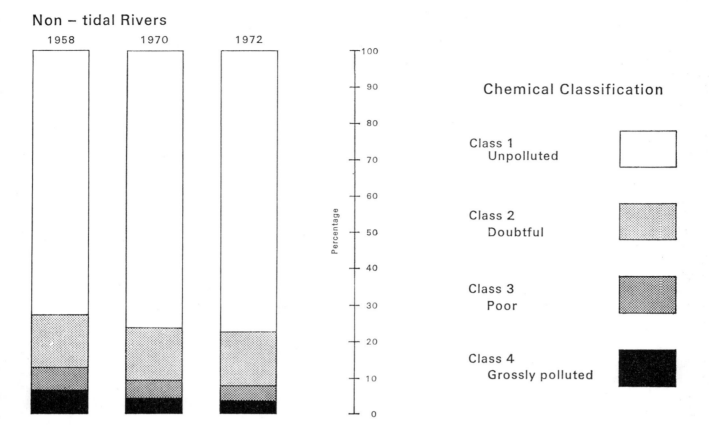

Chemical Classification

Class 1
Unpolluted

Class 2
Doubtful

Class 3
Poor

Class 4
Grossly polluted

Tidal Rivers

Canals

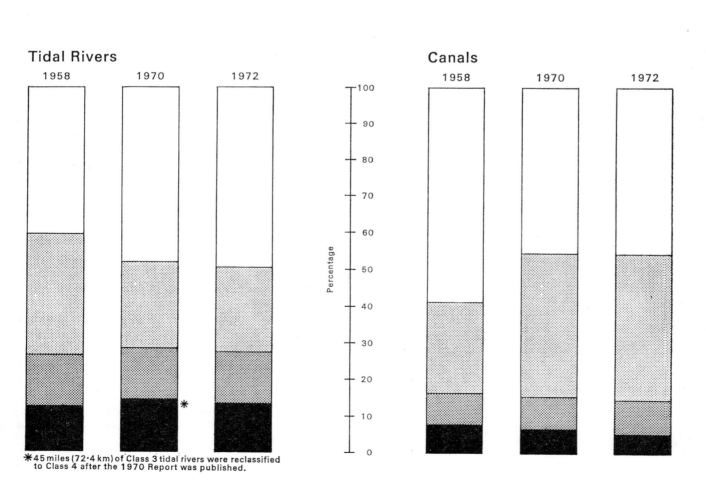

*45 miles (72·4 km) of Class 3 tidal rivers were reclassified
to Class 4 after the 1970 Report was published.

DOE October 1972

recent report is the first, with complete surveys being undertaken periodically.

73 Chapters II-IV emphasised the importance of water quality in relation to the conservation and development of water resources. Water quality and the prevention of pollution must in future be seen as an essential part of water resources planning in its widest sense. The importance of this was well illustrated by Chapter 5 of Volume 1 of the Report on the 1970 survey, which analysed the information supplied by river authorities on those stretches of Class 1 or Class 2 river which might be used as sources for future public water supplies.

Sewage treatment and disposal

74 The problems, and effects of various methods, of sewage disposal were reviewed by the Working Party on Sewage Disposal, which reported in 1970. Most of the Working Party's recommendations have been accepted by the Government*. The Working Party noted that, in 1964/5, a large proportion of a sample of sewage works were discharging effluent which failed to comply with conditions specified in the consents of the river authority**. While this general picture is confirmed by the river pollution survey, there has been some improvement. Volume 2 of the survey shows that 36% of sewage works discharges to non-tidal waters, and 54% of the total quantity of sewage effluent still did not conform to the relevant conditions in 1970. There is still a long way to go. The Government have emphasised the need to keep up the momentum of improvement, and particularly to ensure that it does not slacken pending the necessary legislation to set up the new regional water authorities***. It is estimated that, over the five years starting with 1972/1973, capital works projects to the value of about £980 million (at 1972 prices) will be undertaken by sewerage and sewage disposal authorities.

75 It is also essential to impose appropriate conditions on the discharge of effluent by industry and agriculture. Most trade effluents to public sewers are already controlled under the Public Health Acts, which enable the sewerage authority to prescribe conditions and make charges for the cost of sewage treatment. Where discharge is made direct to a watercourse, the consent of the river authority is required and it is for the discharger to provide the necessary treatment plant to ensure compliance with the conditions imposed by the authority.

Estuaries and the sea

76 The estuaries are the channels through which large quantities of the country's water flow to the sea. For example, approximately one fifth of the country's surface water and effluent drains to the sea through the Humber estuary alone. Moreover, the main estuaries have been major centres of industrial – and in some cases population – growth in recent years.

77 Control of discharges under the Clean Rivers (Estuaries and Tidal Waters) Act 1960 applies only to discharges begun since 1960, or to substantial alterations of pre-1960 discharges. Apart from the Thames estuary (to which all discharges are controlled under the private legislation of the Port of London Authority), unaltered pre-1960 discharges can only at present be controlled if an order is made by the Secretary of State under the Rivers (Prevention of Pollution) Acts 1951-61. Very few such orders have been made. The Department of the Environment and the Welsh Office are conducting a survey of the methods of disposal and treatment of sewage by coastal sewerage authorities. The results are expected to be published early in 1973.

78 The Working Party on Sewage Disposal recommended that full control should be extended to all discharges to tidal rivers and estuaries and to discharges to the sea by drains or pipelines. More recently, the Royal Commission on Environmental Pollution have reported on pollution in estuaries and coastal waters*. They also have recommended that full control should be extended to all discharges to tidal waters and that, pending legislation, river authorities should seek Ministerial orders for this purpose "when they think an estuary is at risk". They suggested that river authorities should establish "pollution budgets" for each major estuary agreed by joint committees of river authorities, local authorities and industry to provide "(say) ten-year plans for the control of pollution" related to the needs and problems of the estuary concerned. They also recommended increased research on estuary problems, including the application of more resources to the development of mathematical models to provide a scientific basic for action. The Government have accepted the large majority of the Commission's recommendations.

79 The Government consider that the most fruitful way of making progress is by co-operation between all the parties concerned. For example, joint consultative machinery, on which the river authorities, local authorities and industry are represented, has been established in relation to the Tees, Mersey and Humber estuaries. In addition, the extension of statutory controls should provide a desirable impetus. The Government has therefore already proposed that Regional Water Authorities should be given full control over all discharges to estuaries and the sea. The Royal Commission have emphasised that this will take time, while "estuaries remain more vulnerable to pollution than any other part of the British environment". They have therefore recommended that the existing authorities should be urged to take action under present legislation**. As they have pointed out, it is open to any river authority – or, indeed, to any other interested person – to apply for an order to control pre-1960 discharges, if they consider there are problems in relation to an estuary within their area which are sufficiently urgent to be unable to await general legislation.

80 The Government have already proposed that "wherever possible the control of discharges to major estuaries should be unified in the hands of a single authority".*** Their proposals for the reorganisation of water services go some way towards this, but there will inevitably remain

---

* DOE Circular 10/72 (Welsh Office 18/72) HMSO.
** "Taken for Granted" paragraph 50 HMSO 1970.
*** DOE Circular 92/71, paragraph 9.

* "Third Report: Pollution in Some British Estuaries and Coastal Waters" Cmnd 5054 HMSO 1972.
** Cmnd 5054, paragraph 19.
*** DOE Circular 92/71, paragraph 5.

situations where control is shared by two, or in some cases three, authorities, where special arrangements will be needed. Control of the tidal Thames has been exercised for several years by the PLA through a committee on which the Essex and Kent River Authorities, the Lee Conservancy Catchment Board, the Greater London Council and the City of London are represented. More recently, a joint committee has been formed by the three river authorities concerned with the Humber.

81 As the Royal Commission have pointed out, one of the first needs in the control of estuarial pollution is to gather together the available information about the estuary concerned and to consider whether further research needs to be done to fill the gaps. Here, there are many techniques which can be used, and the resources of Government Departments have been made available to help. For example, a good deal of work on the development of mathematical models has been, or is being, done in relation to the Thames, the Tees and the Mersey, particularly by the Water Pollution Research Laboratory. Research work has also been done on the Humber and a desk study of pollution in the Severn estuary has been completed by WPRL.

82 Reference has already been made to the contribution of the rivers to marine pollution, and to the UK's role in international work on it. At the United Nations Conference on the Human Environment in June 1972, a World Clean Rivers programme was endorsed; while under the Oslo Convention for the prevention of marine pollution by dumping from ships and aircraft in the North East Atlantic, the UK is pledged to take all possible steps to prevent marine pollution of any kind. The UK has played a leading role in progress towards a global marine dumping convention, which was agreed at an inter-governmental conference in London in November 1972.

83 Sewage sludge is disposed of at sea by some sewage authorities, for example authorities in London, Manchester, Bristol and Southampton. In recent years, proposals have been under consideration by the authorities concerned for a considerable increase in sludge disposal in Liverpool Bay. The former Ministry of Housing and Local Government accordingly established a Working Party to consider the various implications of this, so that adequate evidence was available to ensure a decision to be taken. Their report was published in September*. It concluded that, while further work and continued monitoring will be needed, increased dumping would not be harmful. Even if it were eventually increased sixfold, it would hardly affect the marine environment. It would cause no health risk to bathers and yachtsmen; it was highly improbable that sludge residues from the disposal ground would make any significant contribution to the near shore water, and the amenity value of sandy beaches was therefore unlikely to be affected. The report will be taken into account by Ministers in the event of an application from any of the authorities concerned.

Pollution legislation

84 Apart from the control of discharges to estuaries and the sea, there are other areas where the legislation controlling water pollution needs to be tightened up. The Government have now put forward for consultation proposals for:—

The publication of information relating to discharges or applications for consent, in the light of the recommendation of the Royal Commission*.

The further protection of underground water and prevention of accidental pollution, with powers for river authorities to take action where they foresee a danger of pollution.

Full control of trade effluent discharges to public sewers.

Control of discharges of water raised from working mines and investigation of the problems of pollution from disused mines.

Control of pollution from boats, particularly from sanitary appliances.

Proposals are also being prepared for increases in the penalties for pollution offences.

85 Both the Royal Commission and the unofficial working party on the control of pollution have considered the problems arising from new products or processes. The Royal Commission have recommended an "early warning system" to assess their environmental impact and the waste treatment and disposal problems they may raise**. For some products, eg synthetic detergents, voluntary machinery already exists. The Government have agreed in principle that a system is needed and the Department of the Environment have had preliminary discussions with the CBI on the form which it might take.

Monitoring

86 Monitoring is necessary to determine pollutant levels and the condition of aquatic fauna and flora and, more specifically, to ensure that discharge conditions are being complied with or that water is fit for the uses for which it is required. The work on the river pollution surveys of the rivers of England and Wales in 1958, 1970 and 1972 has already been summarised in paragraph 72. The survey will be periodically updated. In addition, arrangements are under consideration for a national co-ordinated scheme to monitor a range of physical, chemical and biological parameters in all the major UK rivers. Such a scheme might eventually form part of a European river monitoring programme. Local authorities monitor discharges to their sewers to ensure that consent conditions are being met and hence to protect their sewers and sewage works and to ensure that the final discharge to the river is satisfactory. Similarly, river authorities monitor discharges to their rivers at varying intervals, depending on the volume and composition of the discharge. They also monitor rivers directly to determine the oxygen demand, oxygen content and, in many cases, various other parameters including

---

* "Out of Sight, Out of Mind" Report of a Working Party on Sludge Disposal in Liverpool Bay. HMSO 1972.

* "Second Report – Three Issues in Industrial Pollution" paragraphs 3-10, Cmnd 4894. HMSO 1972.
** Second Report, Cmnd 4894, HMSO 1972, paragraphs 11-18.
*** Paragraph 71.

levels of trace elements. Many river authorities employ biologists to conduct surveys of aquatic life, both as a means of assessing the condition of the river and as a guide to levels of trace contaminants in the river, since contaminants such as toxic metals are often concentrated at measurable levels in plants, fish, invertebrates or birds. Underground waters are also monitored by river authorities. In addition to these regular surveys, the Water Pollution Research Laboratory, Water Research Association or DOE's Directorate General Water Engineering from time to time conduct special surveys to determine whether certain other pollutants should be included in routine monitoring programmes.

87 This chapter indicates the progress which has already been made and the further measures which are being taken to tighten up control of river pollution so as to clean up our rivers. While progress has been made, the river pollution survey shows the extent to which further improvement is still needed. Volume 2 of the 1970 survey report estimates that the "expenditure required to bring all discharges of sewage and industrial effluent up to the standards river authorities expect to impose by 1980 would be about £610 million (at constant 1970 prices)". Moreover, this does not include expenditure on sewerage or on the replacement of worn-out equipment, which the report estimates "could well account for as much again"*. This is a major challenge, but one which the new authorities should be able to meet.

---

* DOE Circular 64/72 (Welsh Office 127/72), paragraphs 9-10.

VI Land Drainage and Fisheries

Land drainage

88 Land drainage in the wider sense is concerned with getting unwanted water off the land safely away to the sea. In agricultural terms, it involves the control of soil moisture by both under-drainage and irrigation to create the optimum conditions for crop growth. In flooding terms, it involves the appropriate protection of both urban property and agricultural land.

89 Land drainage is vital to an efficient agriculture. Of the 27 million acres of farmland in England and Wales, about 7 million acres now have under-drainage systems and it is estimated that about a further 7 million acres could become more productive by the introduction of under-drainage systems. The Strutt Report* urged the speeding up of both field drainage and the arterial drainage on which so much successful field drainage depends. In short, better land drainage is critical to the farming infrastructure which, in view of the need for agricultural expansion, is a major economic interest in view of our impending EEC membership.

90 The importance of flood protection – both fluvial and tidal – again needs no emphasis. In some parts of the country, urban and agricultural development alike would become impossible without adequate land drainage.

91 As the Central Advisory Water Committee recognised, there are no outstanding problems of organisation or future policy relating to land drainage, flood protection and sea defence which in themselves call for any change in the existing arrangements. However, the reorganisation of the other water services is so extensive that it is impossible to leave the organisation of land drainage untouched. The essence of land drainage administration is that, both because of its interconnection with agriculture and because of its immediate importance to low-lying areas at risk from flooding, it needs to be locally based. The Government's legislative proposals will therefore require each regional water authority to establish a statutory land drainage committee. A bare majority of its members will be appointed by local authorities, and the remainder by the RWA and the Minister of Agriculture, Fisheries and Food. The committee will be required to submit, through the RWA, schemes for the establishment of local committees, to be based on catchments or groups of catchments, for the approval of the Minister.

92 Regional water authorities will be placed under a new statutory duty to survey the need for the land drainage works in their areas, and to draw up and put into effect a programme for carrying them out. This responsibility will fall to the statutory regional land drainage committee,

* Modern Farming and the Soil, 1970.

which will submit investment programmes through the RWAs to the Minister. For the time being, land drainage activities will continue to be financed by precepts on local authorities and internal drainage boards and, where appropriate, by charges on owners and occupiers of agricultural land, together with Government grants. It is intended, however, that each RWA should be able after a reasonable period, on the recommendation of its regional land drainage committee, to apply to transfer to a system of finance from charges made by the authority on users of water services; and that, if he is satisfied that the change is in the public interest, the Minister of Agriculture, Fisheries and Food, with the agreement of the Secretary of State, should be able to authorise it.

Fisheries

93 Conservation of salmon, trout and freshwater fisheries is a major means not only of ensuring the continued wellbeing of the sport but of safeguarding the important commercial interests involved. Responsibility for this function rests at local level with the river authorities, under the national oversight of the Minister of Agriculture, Fisheries and Food. Apart from the importance of angling as a participatory sport, the national value of fisheries is very high. A recent survey indicated that the angling community spend on average about £80 per head per annum on their sport. In England and Wales the sale value of salmon fisheries, based upon average catches during the last 5 years, is from £500 to £750 per fish caught. Also, a first class salmon fishery can cost £20 a yard of bank to buy and a trout or even a mixed fishery £7 to £10 a yard. Clearly, with increasing demand these values will rise.

94 It is generally agreed that the fisheries functions need to be managed in close conjunction with the other activities affecting rivers, such as abstraction of water, control of pollution and recreational activities. At the same time, this is also pre-eminently a localised function in which it is important to take account of local knowledge as far as possible. Its administration should be designed to provide a flexible basis to take account of the very varied local fishery circumstances to be found in England and Wales. It is therefore proposed to place a duty upon regional water authorities to maintain, improve and develop salmon, trout and freshwater fisheries and to make satisfactory administrative arrangements to ensure that there is full consultation with fishery interests in their areas. It is proposed that each RWA should establish a fisheries committee responsible for planning the development of fisheries and of advising broadly on the major proposals affecting them in the authority's area, and upon its fisheries

budget. The committee might consist of members appointed by the authority, the Minister of Agriculture, Fisheries and Food and others. In addition, it is envisaged that there will continue to be local committees, possibly on the basis of the previous river authority areas, to reflect local views to the fisheries committee.

VII Use of Water Space

95 One of the important characteristics of a river is that it may be used for a number of different purposes at the same time. These include water supply, the disposal of waste, land drainage and flood protection, all of which are discussed elsewhere in this report. This chapter is concerned with the recreational and amenity uses of water.

96 In recent years there has been a rapid growth in the recreational and amenity use of water space, not only on inland waterways but also on reservoirs and gravel pits, where there was practically no demand a quarter of a century ago. The development of the modern economy, which has brought a higher standard of living and an increased amount of leisure time for most of the population, has led to an enormous increase in the demand for water-based facilities. It is estimated that there are now some 6 million people in Britain who regularly engage in inland water-based leisure activities, and this figure does not include ramblers, campers, bird watchers and other casual users of water space. Each summer weekend, there are probably more people in boats on inland waters than there are on all the professional football terraces on an average winter weekend. The number of sailing clubs affiliated to the Royal Yachting Association has grown from 400 to 1600 over the last 20 years; canoe clubs have increased from 12 to 350 and rowing clubs have doubled. Last – but far from least – there are estimated to be about 3 million anglers.

97 In addition, there are millions of other people more indirectly interested in the benefits which water space can provide in the improvement of the environment. Water provides a natural focus of attention for those interested purely in a day out in the country and in quiet enjoyment of the countryside. Much of this is associated with the growth of motoring. Not merely does the motor vehicle make it possible for all those taking part in water sports to travel ever further in pursuit of their interests, but it does much to explain the growth of general interest, the increasing need for the provision of parking spaces and picnic areas, and so on. If this rapidly growing demand is to be properly met, with a balanced provision of facilities for all the differing – and sometimes conflicting – interests concerned, it will be necessary for the amenity and recreational use of water space – including land beside or near water – to be both protected and promoted at regional and national levels. The Government have therefore announced that it is their policy that the best use must in future be made of rivers, lakes, canals, reservoirs, gravel pits and other man made stretches of water for the wider benefit of sport, recreation, conservation and amenity in the widest sense and have put forward proposals for achieving this.

Present position

98 Inland waters are currently owned or controlled by a wide range of authorities, both public and private. The British Waterways Board and some river authorities and harbour authorities are statutory navigation authorities for inland waters. Most publicly owned reservoirs are the responsibility of statutory water undertakers, including water companies, though others are being or may be constructed by river authorities. Other waters are owned or controlled by local authorities and many other waters remain under private control.

99 Considerable progress has already been made in developing the use of water space. For example, the use of rivers and canals has been developed by navigation authorities. In 1971, some 14,000 craft were licensed to cruise on the British waterways network and almost 13,000 craft to use the non-tidal Thames. Statutory water undertakers, through the British Waterworks Association and with the advice of the Institution of Water Engineers, have reviewed the recreational and amenity use of their reservoirs. While safeguards are still necessary in the interests of water quality, particularly on direct supply reservoirs, it has been possible to develop the use of reservoirs considerably further. Moreover, fears of water contamination apply much less strongly to the use of regulating reservoirs for these purposes. In a survey undertaken in 1970, about half the statutory water undertakings had already extended the facilities for the use of their reservoirs or proposed to do so.

100 Existing arrangements already enable the Countryside Commission, the Sports Council and the Regional Sports Councils and the Tourist Boards to encourage recreational and amenity use of water space, and the Nature Conservancy has responsibilities for wild life conservation. Local authorities have an important role in making provision for recreation and amenity both in their structure plans and also in practical terms by either providing facilities or by supporting and assisting particular local projects. The Government have emphasised the importance of continued local authority participation in this respect, in close liaison with the new water authorities.

New arrangements

101 The Government's proposals for the reorganisation of water services are intended to provide the opportunity to build on and strengthen these existing arrangements. The reorganisation itself will bring together the waters for which river authorities and statutory water undertakers are currently responsible under the comprehensive control in each region of a single water authority. The Government have proposed that each authority should

have a statutory duty to make the best use of the waters under its control for recreation and amenity in its widest sense and that it should have the necessary powers to enable it to do so.

102 Each authority will need to undertake a comprehensive review of the water space for which it is responsible and to prepare and carry out plans for the development of those waters for the purposes of sport, recreation, conservation and amenity. The aim is to achieve a balanced provision of facilities, taking account of all the interests involved and the character of the waters concerned. In developing its plans, each regional water authority will need – as it will in respect of its other functions – to take account of the structure plans of the local authorities concerned ; and the provision of facilities will, of course, be subject to the normal planning procedures. The RWAs will work in close consultation with the Countryside Commission and the appropriate regional Sports Council or Councils ; with the local authorities within its region, and with the Regional Tourist Board or Boards concerned with its area.

103 Sections 101 and 102 of the Water Resources Act 1963, relating to the preservation of amenity, public rights of access and land of special natural interest should apply to the new authorities. They will also be under the obligation set out in section 11 of the Countryside Act to have regard to the desirability of conserving the natural beauty and amenity of the countryside in the exercise of their functions. Not only will this mean that RWAs will give particular attention to the location of new reservoirs, but they will also accept a responsibility for sensitive landscape and design treatment for work which they carry out. Tree planting beside reservoirs and in association with flood relief schemes, or the employment of landscape architects on the staffs of the RWAs, are examples of ways in which this might be achieved.

104 The Government's legislative proposals will also provide for the formation, under the aegis of the National Water Council, of a *Water Space Amenity Commission.* The Commission will advise the Secretary of State, the Council and the Water Authorities on the efficient performance by the authorities of their functions relating to the recreational and amenity use of water in England. It will consist of the chairmen of the authorities and members appointed by the Secretary of State, and will provide a forum in which the RWAs will be able to discuss common problems and concert common policies in relation to recreation and amenity.

Recreation in Wales

105 In Wales, the Welsh National Water Development Authority will be responsible for the amenity use of water space in association with the Sports Council for Wales, the Wales Tourist Board and the Countryside Commission. In its report on 'Water in Wales'*, the Welsh Council placed particular emphasis upon the need to develop the recreational and tourist uses of the Principality's water resources. The Government propose that the Welsh authority should have the statutory duty to prepare a plan for the use of water in Wales for these purposes and that it

should have power to implement this plan. In the Upper Severn Basin the plan will be formulated in conjunction with the Severn/Trent Regional Water Authority and executed by that authority in accordance with a scheme to be agreed by both authorities.

---

* Cmd 3334, HMSO 1970.

VIII Research and Development

106 A soundly based research and development programme is an essential part of a comprehensive water policy. The earlier chapters of this report have already illustrated some of the problems calling for research and development. The massive scale of development and investment needed in water services makes it essential to undertake research and development work into the most efficient ways of meeting the increasing demand for water and effluent disposal. Equally, the social factors involved call for a careful evaluation of the different methods of meeting the demand for water discussed in Chapter III. Chapter IV gives a clear indication of the needs in relation to water quality and Chapter V discussed the mounting importance being attached to resolving the problems of pollution and of cleaning up the country's rivers. In addition, there are problems relating to recreation and amenity and to the ecological implications of various developments. This all adds up to a need for a major research programme. But if all these problems are to be tackled properly, without wasting manpower and financial resources, there is also a need for effective co-ordination and control of the programme.

107 There are at present a number of bodies concerned with research and development in this field. The Department of the Environment is concerned with research in relation to all aspects of water services and management, except land drainage and fisheries. The Department supports a major research and development programme both through its Directorate General Water Engineering (whose programme is currently running at about £1 million a year) and its research establishments: the Water Pollution Research Laboratory, whose work is entirely in this field; the Hydraulics Research Station, the Building Research Establishment and the Transport and Road Research Laboratory, all of which are concerned with particular aspects. The other main bodies concerned with research relating to the water cycle or the use of water are the Water Resources Board, whose expenditure is borne on the Department's vote, and the Water Research Association which is grant-aided by the Department. The Ministry of Agriculture, Fisheries and Food are responsible for ensuring that there is adequate research on land drainage and fisheries; the Natural Environment Research Council are involved at a number of points, and some research is also undertaken or commissioned by the Welsh Office, the Department of Health and Social Security and the Medical Research Council. The total value of the research programmes for which all these bodies are responsible is over £5 million a year. The activities of these bodies are summarised in the Appendix to this report.

Co-ordination

108 While each of the bodies described in the Appendix has its own particular responsibilities, it is not possible to define the boundaries between them in any precise way. For example, while the Water Resources Board is primarily concerned with the quantitative assessment of water resources, questions of water quality will be relevant to the use of particular resources. Similarly, both the WRB and the WRA are studying aspects of the potential for the artificial recharge of aquifers. The different research programmes will also depend upon common techniques. For example, WRB, WRA and WPRL all depend increasingly upon the techniques of operational research and of economic analysis in their various studies. It is therefore important to try to avoid unnecessary overlap between the various bodies and to ensure the efficient use of the resources available. This is the basis of the Government's proposals for the future organisation of water research and development.* Steps have been taken, however, to try to ensure that these objectives are achieved within the present organisation.

109 First, there is close contact between the various bodies, and exchanges of membership between the various committees controlling them. For example, officers of the Department of the Environment, the WPRL and the Water Resources Board are members of the council and/or research advisory committee of the Water Research Association. Similarly, the Government Departments concerned, the UKAEA and the WRA are members of the Water Resources Board's committees concerned with desalination.

110 Secondly, the Department of the Environment has established a Water Supply and Waste Disposal Research Requirements Committee which is responsible, on the "customer/contractor" principle, for the programme within the Department's direct control, including the relevant work of the WPRL and the Hydraulics Research Station, and of other Government laboratories, such as the Building Research Establishment, which may be less directly involved. These establishments and the Water Resources Board are represented on the Committee.

111 Thirdly, where appropriate, research is undertaken by two or more of the bodies concerned on a collective basis. Notable among these has been the Trent Research Programme, co-ordinated by the Water Resources Board. Its object was to determine the different ways in which the river Trent, its tributaries and other waters concerned might be used to satisfy the future demands in the area or

---

* See paragraph 115 below.

elsewhere for water for domestic, industrial, agricultural and amenity use. One of the objectives was to evaluate the costs and benefits of each of these ways as a guide to deciding on the most efficient solution. The programme involved the Water Resources Board, the Water Pollution Research Laboratory, the Water Research Association, the Departments of the Environment (DGWE) and of Health and Social Security, the University of Birmingham, the Trent and Lincolnshire River Authorities, the Upper Tame Main Drainage Authority and the Local Government Operational Research Unit.

112 Another example has been the work of the Working Party concerned with the study of the feasibility of substantially increasing the rate of dumping of sludge in Liverpool Bay.* This is a multi-disciplined group chaired by the Department of the Environment (Directorate General Water Engineering) and includes representatives of other Government Departments, the local authorities concerned, Universities, the Sea Fisheries Committee and representatives of the Natural Environment Research Council.

113 Water treatment is also the subject of co-operative research at international level. The prospects for collaborative research on desalination have already been mentioned in paragraph 41 above. Another example is a major project on the physico-chemical treatment of sewage which is being carried out under the auspices of the NATO Committee on the Challenges of Modern Society. In this project, the United Kingdom is collaborating with the United States, France and Germany. The United Kingdom contribution will be the construction of a large pilot plant at a main drainage authority works, together with supporting research by the Water Pollution Research Laboratory.

Scotland and Northern Ireland

114 While this report as a whole relates only to water services in England and Wales, there is a considerable common interest throughout Britain in relation to research and development. Many of the activities described in the Appendix are relevant to water services in Scotland and Northern Ireland. In particular, the Scottish Development Department have their own research programme, and operate in much the same way as the Department of the Environment but their work is largely through local authorities and river purification boards. They are also represented on the Research Requirements Committee mentioned in paragraph 110, so as to maximise the common benefits and avoid overlap between programmes.

Future organisation

115 The reorganisation of water services will make it possible to reduce the present fragmentation of responsibility for research and development. The Government have proposed that a substantial part of the work that needs to be done for the water services industry should be grouped in a new industrial research centre covering all the functions of the new authorities. Its Council would include representatives of the RWAs, the industry in Scotland and Northern Ireland, equipment manufacturers

and Government. They would all provide funds, and could place contracts with the new centre. The Government would also need to maintain its own research capability, and to ensure that there was a comprehensive research programme covering the whole water and pollution field. The precise arrangements are being worked out in consultation with those concerned.

* See paragraph 83.

IX Reorganisation of Water Services

116 The previous chapters illustrate the wide range of demands upon our rivers and other inland waters, the rapid present and forecast growth of those demands and the extent to which they are interconnected. The rivers themselves are natural land drainage channels and are essential to water supply, waste disposal, fisheries, recreation and amenity. At the moment, these functions are the responsibility of a large number of bodies of different types: river authorities, statutory water undertakers and local authorities. In order to cope with rising demand, most of them are faced with the need for a massive investment programme for the remainder of the century. Moreover, these different demands need to be reconciled as far as possible and, where irreconcilable conflict arises, decisions will have to be taken on the merits of each case to determine the priorities.

117 The Government have concluded that this can best be achieved by setting up a small number of large, multi-purpose authorities to manage the rivers on an integrated systems basis. They have announced their intention to introduce in the 1972/3 session of Parliament a Bill to establish 9 Regional Water Authorities for England and a Welsh National Water Development Authority. The areas for which the Government propose they should be responsible are shown in Map 2. Each authority will take over the responsibilities of river authorities, of water undertakers and of local authorities in relation to sewerage and sewage disposal for its area. They will thus be responsible for water resources and supply; sewerage and sewage disposal; the prevention of pollution; land drainage and flood protection; fisheries; and the recreational and amenity use of their water space, and in some cases for navigation. Between them, they will employ some 75,000 staff, their annual revenue will be about £350 million and their investment budget about £300 million per annum.

Central organisation

118 Responsibility for planning at national level and the development of a national strategy for all aspects of water resources will be primarily a matter for the Government Departments concerned – the Department of the Environment and the Welsh Office in relation to water, sewerage and sewage disposal, river pollution and recreation; and the Ministry of Agriculture, Fisheries and Food in relation to land drainage, flood protection and fisheries. The Government have said, however, that the development of a national strategy does not make it necessary to interpose a national body between Ministers and the RWAs. It is recognised that the Water Resources Board have played an invaluable role in a critical period of development of water services. But the need for such a

body arose from the existence of 29 river authorities. Given the small number of water authorities which will exist in the future, this will no longer be necessary.

119 Moreover, the scope of central planning will have to be broader than the Water Resources Board's planning function, which has been limited by its terms of reference under the 1963 Act. It will need to bring together planning of the augmentation of water resources, water quality and the prevention of water pollution. It is therefore proposed to establish within the Government service a Central Water Planning Unit, which will absorb the planning division of the WRB. The Unit will have an independent role, and will provide advice and a common service to the Government Departments, the National Water Council (see next paragraph) and the RWAs, and the results of its work will be freely available to all of them. The proposed new central arrangements for research and development are summarised in paragraph 115 above.

120 The Government consider, however, that there is a need for a consultative and advisory body at national level. They therefore propose to establish a National Water Council, consisting of representatives of the RWAs and of other members, which could draw together the advice of those concerned on matters of common interest and act as a link between the Government and the authorities on general issues. Where appropriate, it will also be able to provide services for the regional authorities on a collective basis.

Finance and economics

121 If the objectives are to be met, the new authorities must not only manage efficiently a massive programme of investment, but must charge for water services in such a way that full value is obtained from the resources involved. It will still be necessary, at the least, to raise sufficient in charges to meet revenue expenditure. The scale of investment programmes will need to be larger in future. This is partly a consequence of the steadily increasing growth in demand for water. In addition, supply and disposal costs per unit are likely to rise in real terms. It will be increasingly necessary to draw on water sources which are more expensive to exploit or treat, or more distant, or both; while rapidly developing technology often results in new industrial effluents which can be more difficult to treat. The increasing size of the investment programme that is in prospect makes it all the more important that charging systems should be so managed as to avoid the risk of over investment and that effective techniques of investment appraisal should be used.

122 The method of financing water services (other than

land drainage*) would in any case require review, since the new authorities will be established by amalgamating a number of existing authorities with different methods of finance at the moment. These include direct charges for water abstraction and charges by quantity for water supply to industry and agriculture; water rates (a form of charge) for domestic water supplies, general rates for sewerage and sewage disposal services; and Exchequer grants for certain purposes. The regional water authorities will be called upon to integrate the various systems within their areas and will have to produce a rationalised system of finance and investment.

123 A good deal of work remains to be done in formulating economic and financial objectives for the authorities, working these out and in deciding how to meet them. Clearly, the authorities must employ in the most efficient manner both the resources they inherit and the resources they will invest in the expansion of water services. To do this, they will require charging systems which ensure that demand for their services — and hence investment — is not exaggerated by supplying services at prices which are too low in relation to the value of the resources used. Secondly, they will require techniques of investment appraisal which ensure that demand is met in the most efficient way, with due regard to the timing of investment. Thirdly, in addition to pursuing appropriate pricing and investment policies, the authorities will need to ensure that revenue is sufficient to balance recurrent expenditure over a period of years. And in all probability they will, like the nationalised industries, require target rates of return on capital employed. A careful study will need to be made of what rate should be set, how assets should be valued for this purpose, what basis should be used for depreciation charges, and how far investment should be financed from internal resources. As soon as the new structure is established — and before the regional water authorities take over their responsibilities — the Government will wish to discuss with them, probably through the National Water Council, the problems involved and how they can best be tackled. Meanwhile, the Department of the Environment has already put in hand a study of financial objectives and of the appropriate relationships of charges to costs. Secondly, a working party has been established, including among its membership representatives of the water industry, to advise on the general principles to be followed in preparing annual estimates and accounts, to facilitate comparisons of performance, and to provide tools of management.

124 The new authorities will need to review the various charging systems in their areas and, where appropriate, to rationalise them. This process, which will take some time, will need to be undertaken in the light of the study of charges and costs referred to in the previous paragraph. In particular, charges should not be seen just as a way of getting the necessary revenue and allocating the cost fairly among the different users of the service. Their function is more important than that. To ensure an optimum use of the available resources, users must be aware of the cost of supplying the water which they use. The best way

of ensuring this is to relate the charge for the water used directly to the cost of that water. For industrial users who are already charged by volume, the means of relating charges to costs exists (though a great deal of work remains to be done before charges can be set at levels which are 'right' in this sense). For domestic consumers the position is different. They are normally charged according to the rateable value of the dwelling. This method is open to the criticism that it is unfair — in that a large family in a small house will normally pay less than a small family in a large house — and that it does nothing to encourage economy in the use of water. One possible solution might be to meter domestic water supplies and charge by the volume used, like the supply of gas or electricity, but this is open to the counter criticisms that meters are costly, and that charging for water in this way may have effects that are detrimental to public health. Similar arguments exist with regard to the use of the public sewerage system. Since use of this system is related at least in part to the volume of water used, a single meter could be used as a basis for both water and sewerage charges. By spreading the cost of metering over two services, this would reduce one of the objections to metering. These arguments are discussed more fully in the consultation paper on economics and finance issued by the Department of the Environment and the Welsh Office.

125 The balance of the economic and social arguments for and against such metering is, however, by no means clear cut, and depends entirely on the individual circumstances obtaining in an area. A research project is already in hand on this question, the results of which will be made available to the new authorities when the study is completed. Meanwhile, the Government's legislative proposals will include sufficiently wide powers to enable regional water authorities to charge for their services on the most appropriate basis, including power to charge by metered quantity wherever this may be appropriate. This proposal has been widely misunderstood, and has been interpreted by many as an intention on the Government's part to introduce universal metering. The intention is to ensure only that the powers are available, should a particular authority decide that, for some particular area, the balance of the economic and social arguments (including any possible impact on public health) is such that it is appropriate to charge on this basis.

Grants

126 Water supply and sewerage services are normally financed from charges and rates respectively. Grants are paid to local authorities, however, under the Rural Water Supplies and Sewerage Acts for the provision of piped water and main drainage in rural areas. The Government have proposed that following reorganisation these grants should be paid to regional water authorities when they provide such facilities in similar circumstances in rural localities. Under the present arrangements county councils are liable to make contributions towards schemes receiving Exchequer grant. This liability will come to an end with reorganisation. The general future of rural water supplies and sewerage grants will be reviewed when the study of the financial objectives of the new authorities

---

* See paragraph 92 above.

has been completed.

The short term

127 While the Government intend to proceed urgently with their proposals for reorganisation, this will inevitably take time. Legislation cannot be introduced until early in the winter, and is unlikely to be enacted before the summer of 1973. The Government then hope to set the authorities up as quickly as possible, so that they have some months to plan the steps they need to take before they take over their assets and start to exercise their functions on 1 April 1974. During this interim period, the new authorities will only be able to deal with the most urgent organisational and financial questions, and these issues will inevitably continue to occupy much of their time even after vesting date.

128 Meanwhile, given the urgency of the problems discussed in this report, it is essential to avoid any slowing down in the current investment programme designed to meet immediate problems and the needs of the nearer future. The Govermnent have already encouraged the existing authorities to keep up the momentum in the time remaining before the regional water authorities take over*. Machinery has also been established to smooth the transition to the new organisation and to enable the new authorities to pick up the threads as quickly as possible. When they take over, they will need to proceed with urgent schemes and plans which are already at various stages in the pipeline. In order to assist in this, the Department of the Environment and the Welsh Office are in close touch with the existing authorities to obtain the necessary material to provide an administrative and technical brief for the regional authorities when they take office.

---

* DOE Circular 92/71, paragraph 9. HMSO.

Department of the Environment
Welsh Office
December 1972.

Appendix   Research and Development on Water Services

1 In carrying out their functions under the Water Resources Act 1963, the *Water Resources Board* are empowered to carry out such research as they consider necessary or expedient. Since their formation, and in collaboration with the river authorities and other interested bodies, they have developed an extensive research programme, some of which is carried out by the Board themselves, often jointly with river authorities, and some of which is contracted out.

2. The Board's research and development expenditure for 1971/72 was approaching £700,000. This includes £300,000 contributed to river authorities for work of an experimental nature, mostly carried out in conjunction with the Board. The bulk of the Board's expenditure is approximately equally divided under three headings :—

a *New types of resources*
As indicated in Chapter III, the Board have carried out directly, and also sponsored, research and development work on new techniques. Substantial effort is devoted to controlled groundwater abstraction, and also to the artificial recharge of aquifers, with pilot works operating in Nottinghamshire and in the London Basin. The work on both these subjects is discussed at more length in Chapter III of this report. The Board also have a specific responsibility under the Water Resources Act to advise the Secretaries of State on the prospects for the application of desalination techniques in England and Wales and their second report on this subject was published in December.

b *Operational research*
The board have developed the use of operational research techniques to assist in their planning work and in the detailed hydrological design of water resources schemes. Mathematical models have been designed to produce optimal capital investment programmes to assist in resource allocation decisions. Models have similarly been developed for use in the design and operation of schemes; on river regulation; and as a contribution to the Trent Research Programme described more fully in paragraph 111 of this report.

c *Data acquisition and processing*
The Board's work in this sphere has concentrated on the development of suitable instruments for measurement and recording, the use of telemetry for data transmission and the use of computers for the analysis, evaluation and publication of data.

The Board have also undertaken research into the ecological effects of water resources projects and studies on the demand for and use of water, including the evaluation of recreational benefits, and studies of problems in engineering design and construction.

3 Water undertakers and river authorities, consultants, plant manufacturers, industrial users, educational establishments and others interested in research problems relating to water supply collectively support the *Water Research Association*. Its main income is derived from subscriptions from members, supplemented by a grant from the Department of the Environment, together with funds for repayment work. The Association has its own laboratories at Medmenham on the River Thames. Its programme is steadily expanding and is currently of the order of £½ million.

4 The Association's programme reflects the interests of its members. It includes quality and quantity aspects of resource evaluation, potability and health aspects and the economics of many stages of water supply. The Association is particularly interested in the chemical composition of rivers as it affects their suitability for water supply. This includes such matters as the likely growth of algae when river water is impounded in a reservoir. The Association is also concerned with problems relating to the treatment of water before it is put into public supply, including the cost and efficiency of treatment processes and their sequence; and with the engineering and biological problems which arise in the distribution of water to the consumer. These interests involve the Association in many of the problems of water quality discussed in Chapter IV. The Association is, for example, undertaking under contract from the Department of the Environment a study using spectrographic techniques for determining trace elements in surface waters.

5 The *Department of the Environment* – mainly through the Directorate General Water Engineering – sponsors research and development projects costing about £1 million a year, small parts of which are included in the expenditure quoted for other bodies. Projects are concerned with the conservation of water, control of environmental pollution and the maintenance of public health. Specific aspects include source development, treatment and distribution of water; sewerage, sewage treatment and disposal; trade effluent control; and appropriate aspects of river management.

6 The research element in projects is carried out under agreements by various research bodies and universities; there being particularly close links with WPRL, HRS and WRA. Development of new techniques and equipment on pilot and full scale plants under normal operating conditions is undertaken in collaboration with local authorities and plant manufacturers. Other projects are concerned with the monitoring of storm sewage and of conditions at

sea outfalls. Where the results of work are likely to be of national rather than purely local value, the Department often sets up projects, participates in the overall direction and contributes a proportion of the costs. Thus full access to any results is obtained for use in its national advisory role. It is intended that information and experience on specific subjects should be prepared in a form suitable for designers and operators in the field. Thus more economical designs of public health works should result from a more complete knowledge of process and plant and the conditions for which they are most suitable. Analyses of capital and operational costs and future trends are undertaken to assist in the assessment of alternative schemes.

7 *The Water Pollution Research Laboratory* is principally concerned with water after it has been used and undertakes studies both of treatment processes and of the effect of pollutants in water. The Laboratory was first established in 1927 under the Department of Scientific and Industrial Research. It was transferred to the Ministry of Technology in 1965 and to the Department of the Environment in 1971. Its ultimate objective is to enable the national expenditure on water pollution control to be spent to the best advantage. Its current annual gross expenditure is about £675,000. The Laboratory is the largest in Europe devoted to research into pollution control and one of the largest in the world. It has been responsible for an important part of current technical knowledge in its field and has played a major role for many years in developing or assisting the development of UK practice, which can itself claim to be well in the vanguard of water pollution control throughout the world.

8 The Laboratory devotes much of its effort to studies of the treatment of waste waters, both in order to improve conventional methods of treatment and to try to develop new ones, such as the physico-chemical treatment of sewage. An important part of this activity is concerned with investigation of methods of treatment and disposal of sewage sludges. A complementary part of the laboratory's programme is concerned with studies of the pollution of river, estuarial or coastal waters and their natural self-purifying capacity. This work is essential in helping to determine the extent to which it is either necessary or desirable to use treatment processes.

9 The *Welsh Office* is concerned with aspects of research into water pollution. It maintains close liaison with faculties engaged in such research in the colleges of the University of Wales, and a working party is currently looking into possible pollution problems in Swansea Bay.

10 The *Ministry of Agriculture, Fisheries and Food* carries out research on salmon and freshwater fisheries, and into the toxicity of effluents to marine organisms at its laboratories in London and Weymouth. Its annual programme is of the order of £¼ million. The Ministry is also responsible for ensuring that adequate research on land drainage, including flood protection, is carried out.

11 Like the WPRL, the *Hydraulics Research Station* was established under DSIR (in 1946) and was transferred first to the Ministry of Technology and then to the Department of the Environment. It deals with such civil engineering problems as flood protection; the silting and scouring of rivers, estuaries and harbours; and beach erosion. Where appropriate, it has been concerned with the construction of physical hydraulic models, eg of the investigations into storage in Morecambe Bay and the Wash. Its annual programme is currently about £0.8 million.

12 The *Institute of Hydrology* is an establishment of the Natural Environment Research Council and is responsible for a national programme of basic hydrological research. Its programme comprises work on the effect of geomorphology and land use on the run-off of rainfall; the evaporation process; the flow, storage and depletion of ground and surface water in the hydrological cycle; factors affecting stream flow models of catchment behaviour; and flood studies.

13 The Hydrogeological Department of the *Institute of Geological Science* undertakes research into the quantitative definition of the role of groundwater in the hydrological cycle. Its studies include the characteristics of aquifers, the distribution and chemical quality of groundwater and the infiltration process.

14 The *Freshwater Biological Association*, funded by NERC, is also concerned more with basic scientific knowledge, primarily about the biological processes in freshwater affecting fish and plant life. A report on the Association's objectives and programme was published earlier in 1972*.

15 The *United Kingdom Atomic Energy Authority* was empowered by the Science and Technology Act 1965 to undertake research and development outside the nuclear field, at the direction of the Minister of Technology (now the Secretary of State for Trade and Industry). The Authority has undertaken a substantial programme of work costing approximately £1¼ million per annum, concerned with the production of fresh water from sea water or brackish water and is currently also investigating the application of some of these processes to the treatment of other water for public supply and to sewage treatment. The Authority advises the Water Resources Board on desalination processes.

16 The *Building Research Establishment* is concerned in research affecting the structural properties of materials, design of dams, earthworks and slopes and other subjects which are relevant to water services. The cost of this part of its programme is over £300,000 per annum. The *Transport and Road Research Laboratory* is undertaking a programme on behalf of the Sewers and Water Mains Working Party, costing about £100,000 per annum.

17 The *Department of Health and Social Security* has recently established a Division of Chemical Contamination of Food and the Environment, and has set up an Advisory Committee dealing with the effects of some environmental pollutants and will link the effects of water pollutants with those ingested in food and from the atmosphere. The *Medical Research Council* has been carrying out work on

---

* "Research in Freshwater Biology". Natural Environment Research Council publications series B, No 3, February 1972.

the effects of hard and soft waters and of trace substances in the body.

18 The Agriculture and Hydrometeorology Branch of the *Meteorological Office* is concerned with problems involving precipitation and evaporation.

Map 1

THE DEMAND FOR WATER

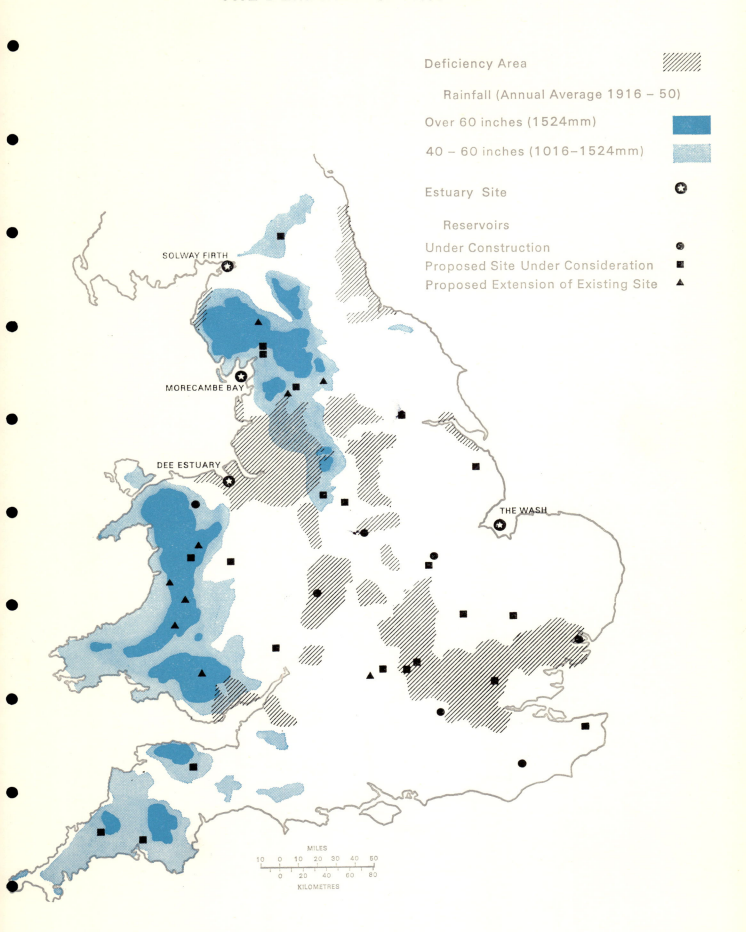

Deficiency Area

Rainfall (Annual Average 1916 – 50)

Over 60 inches (1524mm)

40 – 60 inches (1016–1524mm)

Estuary Site

Reservoirs

Under Construction

Proposed Site Under Consideration

Proposed Extension of Existing Site

SOLWAY FIRTH

MORECAMBE BAY

DEE ESTUARY

THE WASH

MILES
10   0   10   20   30   40   50

0   20   40   60   80
KILOMETRES

DOE October 1972

REGIONAL WATER AUTHORITIES

Areas in England within Welsh
National Water Development Authority

Areas in Wales within
Severn – Trent Water Authority

NORTH EAST

WATER

AUTHORITY

NORTH

WEST

WATER

AUTHORITY

YORKSHIRE

WATER

AUTHORITY

WELSH

NATIONAL

WATER

DEVELOPMENT

AUTHORITY

SEVERN – TRENT

WATER

AUTHORITY

EAST ANGLIA

WATER

AUTHORITY

THAMES

WATER   AUTHORITY

WESSEX

WATER

AUTHORITY

SOUTHERN   WATER   AUTHORITY

SOUTH WEST

WATER   AUTHORITY

MILES

10 0 10 20 30 40   50

0   20   40   60   80

KILOMETRES

Printed in England for Her Majesty's Stationery Office by Albert Gait Ltd, Grimsby.   2/73   G.3339/1

Dd 505869 K40.